THE STORY OF RUTH BADER GINSBURG

A Biography Book for New Readers

Written by
Susan B. Katz

Illustrated by
Micah Player

ROCKRIDGE
PRESS

Thank you to my talented, trailblazer editor, Orli, for your vote of confidence in my writing. We made this book in honor of RBG and all the women who advocate for our equal rights.

For general information on our other products and services or to obtain technical support, please contact our Customer Care Department within the United States at (866) 744-2665, or outside the United States at (510) 253-0500.

Rockridge Press publishes its books in a variety of electronic and print formats. Some content that appears in print may not be available in electronic books, and vice versa.

Series Designer: Angela Navarra

Interior and Cover Designer: Angela Navarra

Art Producer: Hillary Frileck

Editor: Orli Zuravicky

Production Editor: Mia Moran

Illustrations © Micah Player, 2019; © Collection of the Supreme Court of the United States, pp. 46, 49; © Steven Petteway, Collection of the Supreme Court of the United States, p. 47
Author photo courtesy of © Jeanne Marquis

ISBN: Print 978-1-64611-011-7 | eBook 978-1-64611-012-4

R2

Printed in China

CONTENTS

CHAPTER 1 A Trailblazer is Born — 1

CHAPTER 2 The Early Years — 8

CHAPTER 3 A Woman in a Man's World — 15

CHAPTER 4 Fighting for Equality — 22

CHAPTER 5 It's a Woman's World, Too! — 27

CHAPTER 6 Inside the Courtroom — 33

CHAPTER 7 Justice Ginsburg — 39

CHAPTER 8 So . . . Who Was Ruth Bader Ginsburg? — 46

GLOSSARY — 52

BIBLIOGRAPHY — 55

CHAPTER 1
A TRAILBLAZER IS BORN

Meet Ruth Bader Ginsburg

When Joan Ruth Bader came into the world on March 15, 1933, she seemed born to be a fighter. She kicked so much as a baby that her big sister, Marilyn, called her "Kiki." Everyone else called her "Ruth." Ruth was a curious child who loved to read. Among her favorites was *Little Women* by Louisa May Alcott, about a smart, confident girl named Jo and her sisters. Tales of strong girls surely **inspired** Ruth. Maybe Ruth always knew she had an important cause to fight for. Over the course of her life, she was a **trailblazer** in American history.

When she grew up, Ruth became the second woman ever to sit on the **Supreme Court** of the United States, the highest court that makes decisions for the whole country. Ruth helped change many laws to make the United States more fair for women. As a leader, **lawyer**, and **judge**, she fought for **justice** and **equal rights** for all people. Every day, Ruth worked hard to improve the world we live in. What changes did she make, and what inspired her to make them? Let's journey back in time to find out!

Ruth's America

Ruth was born in 1933 in Brooklyn, New York. At that time, boys could grow up to be doctors, lawyers, writers, or anything else they wanted to be, but girls were expected to become wives and mothers. Women who worked outside the home had few options for jobs. Careers like being a nurse, teacher, or secretary were thought of as fitting for women. Most other jobs were off limits!

Women who did have jobs were paid much less than men who were doing the same work. That wasn't the only unfair thing. Even though the first presidential election in the United States took place in 1789, women weren't allowed to vote until 1920—more than 130 years later!

MYTH & FACT

MYTH: Women have always been allowed to go to college.

FACT: Colleges like Harvard, founded in 1636, only allowed men at first. In 1879, women started an all-female college nearby, called Radcliffe.

JUMP IN THE THINK TANK

How would you feel if someone thought you were "bad luck" because of your religion?

During this time, there was also a lot of **anti-Semitism** in the world. Anti-Semitism is the hatred or unfair treatment of Jewish people. Because Ruth's family was Jewish, they experienced anti-Semitism often. Once, on a road trip from New York to Pennsylvania, Ruth and her family drove past a sign that read, "No Dogs or Jews Allowed." Some children on Ruth's street wouldn't invite Jewish kids, like Ruth, over to their houses. Their mothers told them Jewish people brought bad luck.

As terrible as that was, anti-Semitism was much worse in Europe, where Ruth's family was from. Ruth's parents and grandparents were **immigrants** who came to the United States searching for a safer place to live and work.

In 1939, World War II broke out in Europe. The US became involved in 1941, when Ruth was eight years old. American soldiers were sent overseas to join the fighting in World War II against Adolf Hitler, the evil leader of the Nazis in Germany, and Germany's partners, Japan and Italy.

WHEN?

1933 — Ruth is born. Adolf Hitler becomes the leader of Germany.

1934 — Ruth's older sister, Marilyn, dies.

1939 — World War II begins.

1941 — America declares war on Germany.

1945 — World War II ends.

After four long years, on May 8, 1945, Ruth watched as all of New York City danced in the streets to celebrate the victory of America and its partners and the end of the war.

Life was better after the war, but some things hadn't changed. There was still anti-Semitism, and women continued to be treated unfairly. Ruth's mom, however, believed girls could—and should—study and work hard like boys. This early encouragement from her mother inspired her. Ruth would soon find that studying and working hard could change her entire life.

CHAPTER 2

THE EARLY YEARS

Growing Up in Brooklyn

Joan Ruth Bader started kindergarten in 1938. There were so many other kids in her class named Joan that she went by her middle name, Ruth, instead.

Ruth loved to read. Her mother, Celia, took her to the public library every Friday after

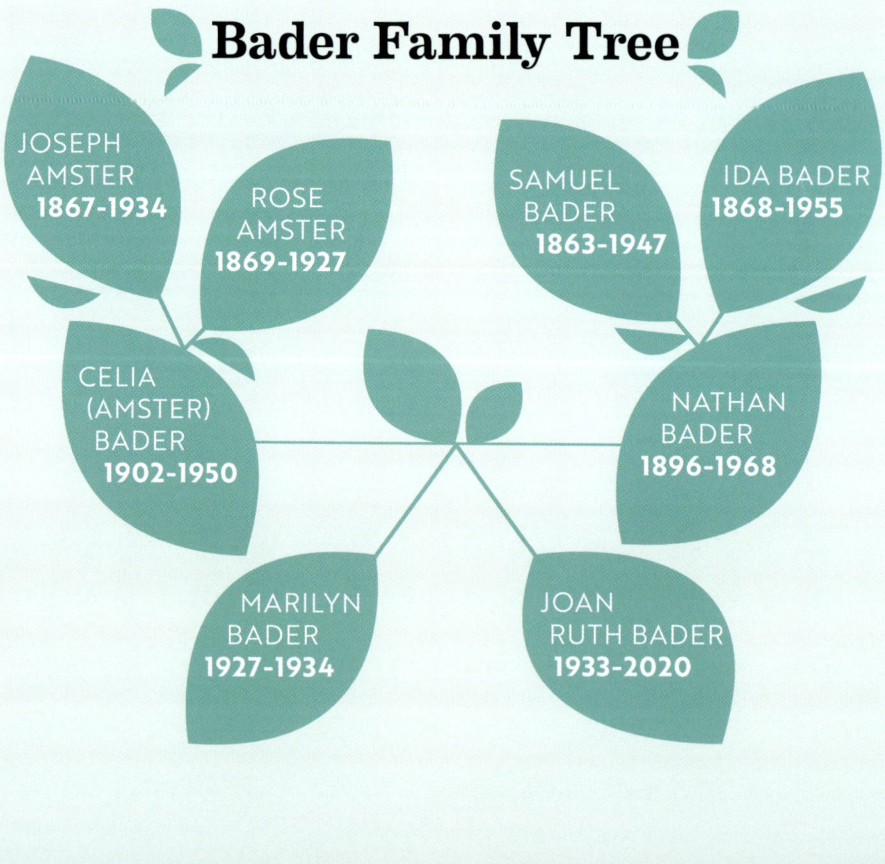

school. Handwriting was harder for Ruth. She was left-handed, and at the time, teachers made all children write with their right hands. This frustrated Ruth to the point of tears. She even got a D in handwriting! After that, she vowed to write only with her left hand. From a very young age, Ruth fought against even the smallest **injustices**.

> "Reading is the key that opens doors to many good things in life. Reading shaped my dreams, and more reading helped me make my dreams come true."

Ruth also didn't think it was fair that girls had to take sewing and cooking while the boys took woodshop. She wished she could have as many choices and opportunities as the boys had at school.

JUMP IN THE THINK TANK

Why do you think certain classes were assigned to boys and other classes to girls? Are there still things that are different for girls and boys today?

Despite her D in handwriting, Ruth was always good with words. She wrote for her middle school newspaper. She was such a strong student that she was even chosen to speak at her high school graduation! Sadly, her mother became very ill with a disease called cancer and died just before Ruth graduated, so Ruth didn't go to her graduation. She stayed home with her father instead.

Blazing into Higher Education

Ruth knew that her mother had wanted her to attend college. So, just a few months after her mother's death in 1950, Ruth started at Cornell University. She was such a strong student that Cornell offered her a scholarship, which means that they gave her money to help pay for her schooling.

At Cornell, Ruth's life changed forever. She met a professor named Robert E. Cushman, who taught her about the country's founding document, the **Constitution of the United States**.

He taught her that the law could help make the world a better place.

Ruth also met Marty Ginsburg during her first year in college. He was one year ahead of her in school. Ruth remembered that he was the first man interested in her for her intelligence. They became friends first, and then dated. Four years later, Marty and Ruth got married. Ruth changed her name to Ruth Bader Ginsburg. She's sometimes called "RBG" for short.

That same year, Ruth graduated from Cornell at the top of her class, with honors. In fact, she was such an incredible student that she was accepted to Harvard Law School in Massachusetts, one of the best law schools in the country. RBG was going to become a lawyer!

Ruth's mom dies. Ruth graduates and starts Cornell.

1950

Ruth graduates Cornell and marries Marty Ginsburg.

1954

WHEN?

CHAPTER 3
A WOMAN IN A MAN'S WORLD

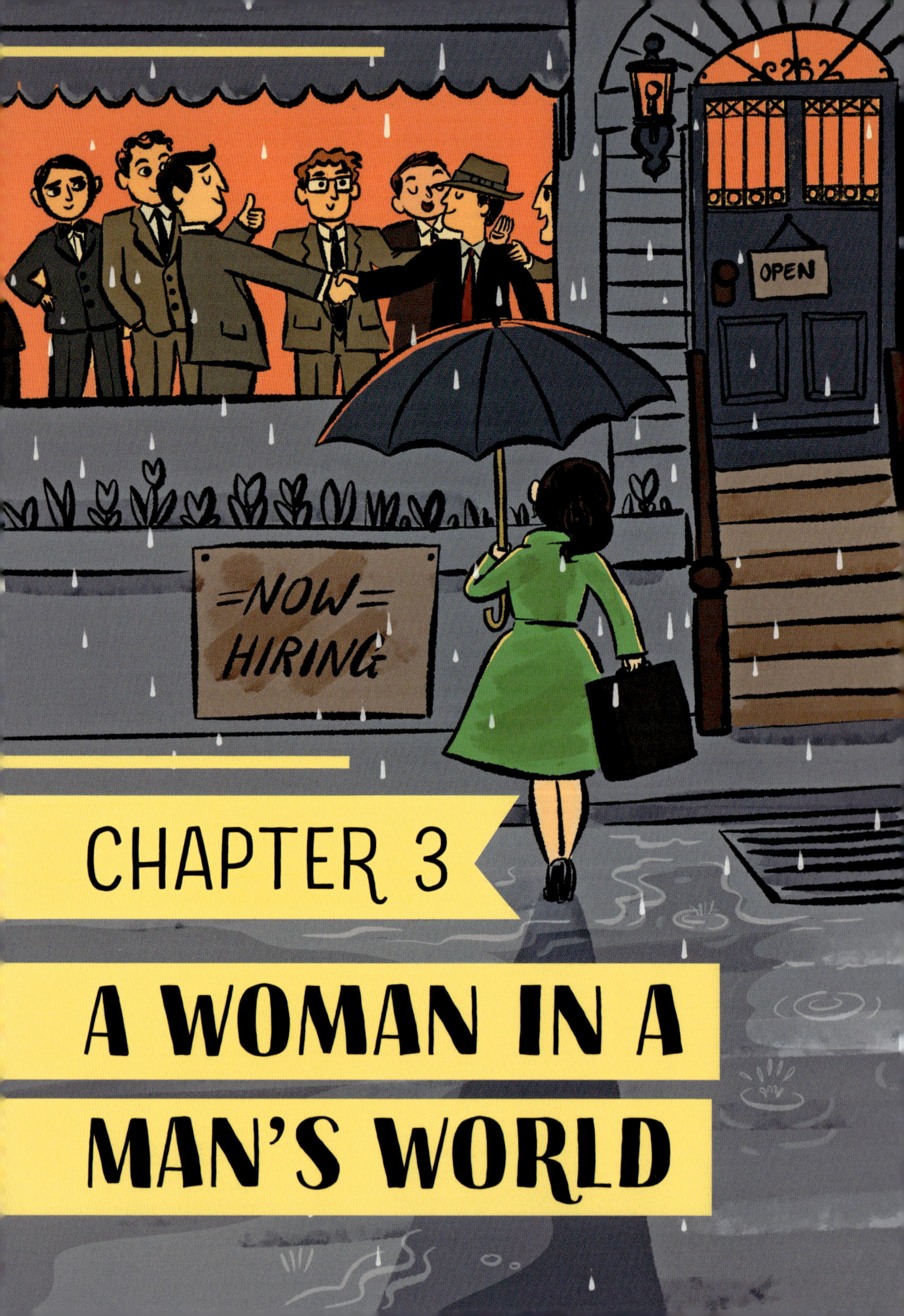

A Big Surprise

Ruth was excited to begin Harvard Law School. Her husband, Marty, had already completed his first year there. Then they got some hard news: A war had broken out in the country of Korea. America needed more soldiers to help fight. So, in 1954, Marty had to take a break from law school to join the army.

The army needed Marty to go to Oklahoma, so he and Ruth moved across the country. Ruth looked for a job there, but most companies would not hire women for the jobs she wanted. This was one form of **discrimination**, or unfair treatment of a certain group of people. In this case, Ruth was treated unfairly because she was a woman.

Finally, Ruth found a job. Soon after, she became pregnant with her first child. When her company discovered she was pregnant, they forced her to take a lower position that paid less money.

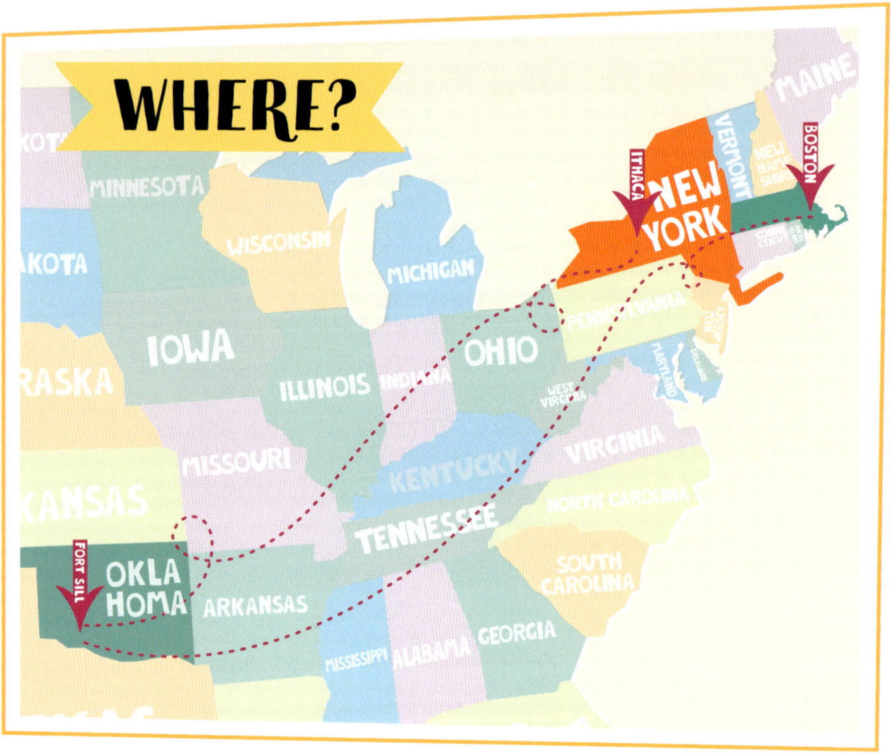

Back on Track at Harvard

Ruth and Marty's first child, Jane, was born in 1955. A year after that, Ruth finally got to go to Harvard Law School. In her class, there were more than 500 men and only nine women!

One of the heads of the law school invited the nine female students to dinner. He asked each of them, "Why are you here, taking the place of a man?" All the women had grades and intelligence equal to their male classmates. Yet he wanted these women to prove, or **justify**, *why* they were as important as the male students. Ruth later learned he had asked for their stories and goals so he could share them with those who doubted that women deserved to be at Harvard Law.

Ruth managed to balance being a new mom and a law student at the same time, but it wasn't easy! Still, she was a born fighter. She studied hard and got excellent grades—even better

JUMP IN THE THINK TANK

If someone asked you to justify your right to learn, how would you answer?

grades than Marty. She was chosen to be on the *Harvard Law Review*, a special law newspaper that only accepts top students.

In 1958, during his final year of law school, Marty became very sick with cancer. Now, Ruth wasn't only going to law school and taking care of her daughter. She was also caring for her ill husband and helping him with *his* schoolwork, in addition to her own! Luckily, Marty got well. After he graduated, he was offered a job as a lawyer in New York City. Ruth changed law schools to keep the family together.

> "My mother told me two things constantly. One was to be a lady, and the other was to be independent. The study of law was unusual for women of my generation."

In 1959, Ruth earned her law degree from Columbia Law School in New York City. She even tied with another classmate for first in her class! She was chosen to be on the *Columbia Law Review,* too, making her the first woman to be on both the *Harvard Law Review* and *Columbia Law Review*.

Despite how hard law schools made it for women, Ruth came out on top. She didn't give up on her dream of being a lawyer because she was living in a man's world. Instead, she chose to change the world.

WHEN?

1955 Ruth and Marty's first child, Jane, is born.

1956 Ruth and Marty move to Boston to attend Harvard.

1958 Marty gets cancer. Ruth starts Columbia in NYC.

1959 Ruth graduates from Columbia.

CHAPTER 4
FIGHTING FOR EQUALITY

JUMP IN THE THINK TANK

Do you think discrimination against women still happens today? If yes, why?

The Unemployable RBG

Even though Ruth was one of the best students at two of the top law schools in the country, it was still almost impossible for her to find a job. Most employers didn't want to hire women, and they *especially* didn't want to hire mothers.

One of the professors from Columbia Law School, Gerald Gunther, called every judge in town to tell them about Ruth, but nobody would hire a woman with a four-year-old daughter. Her grades were excellent, but judges worried she would be too busy taking care of her child to work hard.

Finally, Professor Gunther found someone to give Ruth a chance. He reached out to Judge Edmund Palmieri and begged him to hire Ruth as his clerk. In fact, Professor Gunther vowed to never send another Columbia student to clerk for Judge Palmieri if he didn't hire her. Judge Palmieri agreed to give Ruth the job, but Professor Gunther had to promise that if she didn't work out, he would find Judge Palmieri a male clerk. Professor Gunther agreed. Thankfully, he never needed to replace Ruth. She worked hard for Judge Palmieri and did such a great job that she kept the position for two years. During that time, she learned just how important a judge's decisions can be.

Abroad in Sweden

After working for Judge Palmieri, Ruth traveled to Sweden in 1962 to research how **courts** work in other countries. She

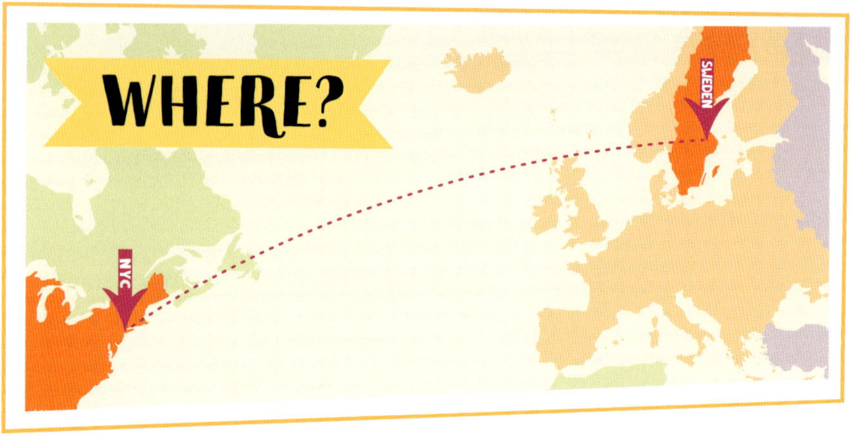

had learned Swedish the previous year. Later, she and a Swedish judge wrote a book about her work there. She even translated Sweden's **Judicial Code**, or laws of the land, into English.

Ruth was inspired by how well women were treated in Sweden. She learned that Swedish women made up 20 to 25 percent of law students.

> "I . . . try to teach through my opinions, through my speeches, how wrong it is to judge people on the basis of what they look like, the color of their skin, whether they're men or women."

One female judge she met in Sweden was eight months pregnant and was allowed to keep working as long as she wanted. Ruth's time in Sweden showed her it was possible for women to have more equal rights than they were given in the United States. The wheels in her head began to turn.

Ruth starts researching Swedish law.

1961

Ruth travels to Sweden.

1962

WHEN?

CHAPTER 5

IT'S A WOMAN'S WORLD, TOO!

Professor Ginsburg

After her work studying Swedish law, Ruth got a job as a law professor at Rutgers University in New Jersey. Finally, Ruth was getting opportunities that only men had been getting for hundreds of years! Ruth knew that Rutgers was paying her less money than male professors doing her same job, but she also knew she couldn't say no to the offer. The university tried to justify its actions, saying she was paid less because her husband had a job, too. Ruth did not think this answer was fair.

When Ruth started teaching at Rutgers in 1963, she was one of only 20 female law professors in the whole country. While teaching there, she became pregnant with her second child. Once again, Ruth tried to hide her pregnancy for fear of being fired.

JUMP IN THE THINK TANK

Standing up for yourself, like Ruth did, can be scary. Sometimes it's easier to stay quiet when unfair things happen. What are some reasons for taking a stand, even when it seems scary?

In 1965, she and Marty welcomed their son, James, into the world.

In 1971, a group of female professors, including Ruth, filed a federal **lawsuit** against Rutgers for discriminating against women. They took the university to court—and they won! Rutgers was told it had to change the amounts it paid to women to match the amounts it paid to men for the same work. Things were starting to change for the better.

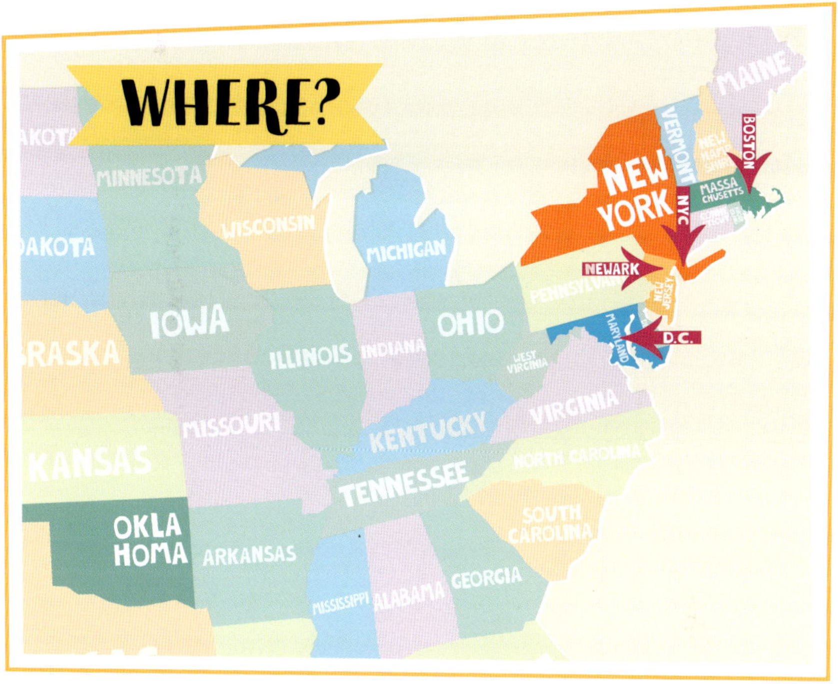

Taking a Stand

In the 1960s, the American Civil Liberties Union (ACLU)—an organization that fights for human rights of all kinds—was hearing from many women and girls who were being treated unfairly. For example, an employee at a school was told to leave work without getting paid while she was pregnant. A female worker at a company was told she couldn't have health insurance because it was only for men. Also, a summer engineering program for sixth graders only allowed boys to sign up.

The ACLU asked Ruth to argue these cases in court for them because she was such a great lawyer. She proudly fought for those women and girls—and she won.

MYTH & FACT

MYTH: **Juries** have always been made up of both men and women.

FACT: Women were not required—and sometimes were not allowed—to serve on juries until the Supreme Court of the United States ruled in 1975 that this was against the Constitution.

Ruth helped lead the women's rights and **social justice** movements in America. By 1971, Rutgers Law School had the second-highest number of female students in the country. Ruth was inspiring other women to become lawyers like her.

Ruth begins teaching law at Rutgers University.

Ruth and Marty welcome their second child, James.

1963

1965

WHEN?

CHAPTER 6
INSIDE THE COURTROOM

Counsel for the American Civil Liberties Union

By 1972, the ACLU had created the Women's Rights Project. Its goal was to fight against **gender discrimination**, or unfair treatment of people because they are male or female. Ruth helped create and direct this project.

> "Fight for the things that you care about, but do it in a way that will lead others to join you."

In her role at the ACLU, Ruth argued six cases before the Supreme Court of the United States—and won five of them! One case was about a man whose mother was sick. If he had been a woman, the government would have given him money to help take care of his mother. But because he was a man, the law said he was on his own. Ruth argued that this discriminated against him because he was male, and she won.

JUMP IN THE THINK TANK

Why do you think it is important for women to have the same rights and job opportunities as men?

With this case, she cleverly showed that gender discrimination hurts men, too. She knew that would matter to the panels of all male judges. She also knew it would help her argue gender discrimination cases for women later on.

At the same time, Ruth became a professor at Columbia Law School. She was the first woman to be hired with **tenure** there, which meant she could work there for as long as she wanted. She also helped write the first legal textbook on gender discrimination.

US District Court of Appeals

Ruth was such a brave and successful lawyer that, in 1980, President Jimmy Carter picked her to be a judge on the United States Court

of Appeals for the District of Columbia. The judges on this court heard cases that had already received a decision at the state level but were being **appealed**. This means people were trying to get judges to change the decision.

Now, Ruth wasn't just a lawyer. She was a judge! Judges do not say if they belong to a particular political party. However, some judges are more **conservative** in their opinions, and others are more **liberal**. Ruth was more liberal. That means she often believed in more help and control from the United States government. Conservatives feel the individual state governments should have more power to make decisions.

During her time on the Court of Appeals, Ruth learned to work with other judges who had different opinions than hers on many issues. For example, Judge Antonin Scalia was much more conservative than Ruth, but they became great friends. They even performed in an opera together!

As a judge, Ruth helped women get more equal pay and **gender equality** when she heard

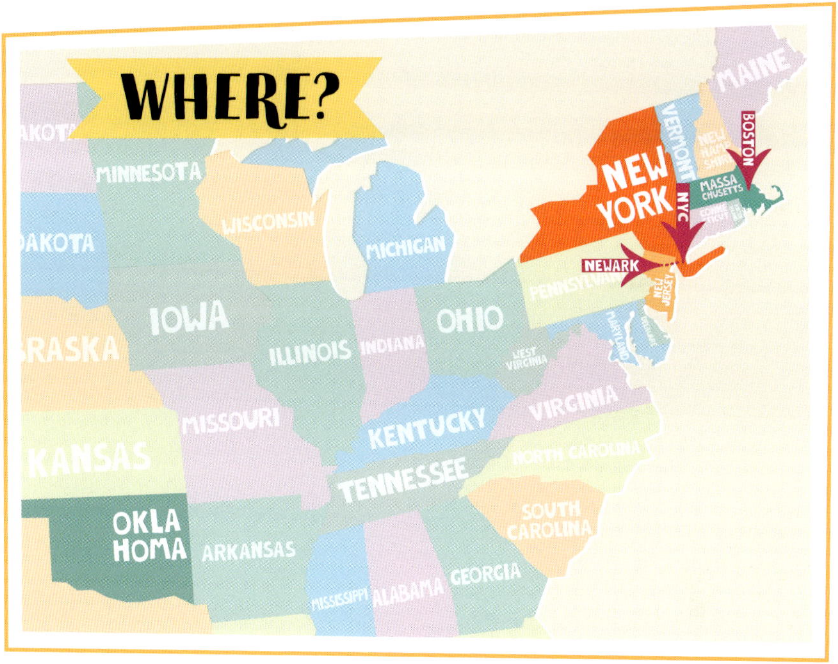

discrimination cases. She also learned that an important part of her job was expressing **dissent**, or an opposing opinion.

Ruth works at ACLU and Columbia Law School.

Ruth becomes a judge for US District Court of Appeals.

1972 **1980** **WHEN?**

CHAPTER 7
JUSTICE GINSBURG

The Highest Court in the Land

The Supreme Court of the United States is the highest court in the nation. Sometimes a legal case is very important and **controversial**, meaning people have very different opinions on how it should be decided. When this happens, a case can move beyond a state's court system and be decided at the national level. It will then be argued in front of the nine justices on the Supreme Court, who will rule on a final decision.

In March 1993, one of these nine justice seats opened up, and President Bill Clinton needed someone to fill it. He got advice from Justice Antonin Scalia, who was then serving on the Supreme Court. President Clinton asked Justice Scalia to help him decide between two men. Justice Scalia told him to choose Ruth Bader Ginsburg instead. President Clinton interviewed Ruth at the White House. He was so impressed by her that he asked her to join the Supreme Court.

Ruth was no longer simply "Kiki" or "RBG." She was now Justice Ginsburg. She became the second woman ever to sit on the Supreme Court, and she was the first Jewish woman to take on this role. After Ruth, two other women joined her on the Supreme Court: Justice Sonia Sotomayor and Justice Elena Kagan.

JUMP IN THE THINK TANK

Why do you think it's important for the Supreme Court to be made up of both men and women as well as people from all different backgrounds?

Sandra Day O'Connor, Justice Sonia Sotomayor, Justice Ruth Bader Ginsburg, and Justice Elena Kagan.

Ruth Dissents

There were many cases where Ruth dissented, meaning she strongly disagreed with the majority ruling of the other justices on the Supreme Court. When Ruth read a dissent, she wore a special collar around the neck of her robe. She also had special collars for when she agreed with the court.

Some issues argued in front of the Supreme Court include a woman's right to make decisions about her own health care and work. One famous case involved a woman named Lilly Ledbetter. She was suing her employer for paying her less because she was female.

Lilly lost her case. The court ruled 5 to 4, saying she waited too long to report that she was being underpaid. Ruth thought that was absurd! In her dissent, she pointed out that women don't usually know they are being paid less, so they can't be expected to report it until they find it out.

After President Barack Obama took office in 2009, the first thing he signed into law was the Lilly Ledbetter Fair Pay Act. Now what happened to Lilly can't happen to anyone else. Ruth helped inspire and write that law!

> People ask me sometimes, 'When will there be **enough women** on the court?' And my answer is, **'When there are nine.'**

In 1999, Ruth found out she had cancer. She continued working through three rounds of cancer treatments. She even went to court the day after Marty died to read a summary of a decision she had made as Supreme Court Justice. She knew that's what Marty would have wanted her to do. Recently, Ruth became sick again. For the first time, she missed a day on the bench in court! Justice Ruth Bader Ginsburg was the most senior liberal judge on the Supreme Court.

True to her trailblazer nature, Ruth kept on fighting for women's rights and human rights in her role as Supreme Court Justice of the United States until the very end. Sadly, on September 18, 2020, Justice Ruth Bader Ginsburg passed away after a long battle with cancer. The nation mourned the loss of RBG: a leader and champion for justice.

WHEN?

1993 — President Clinton asks Ruth to join the Supreme Court.

1999 — Ruth finds out she has cancer.

2009 — President Obama signs the Fair Pay Act.

2010 — Marty dies.

2020 — Ruth Bader Ginsburg dies.

CHAPTER 8

SO . . . WHO WAS RUTH BADER GINSBURG?

Challenge Accepted!

Now that you have learned all about Ruth's life and legacy, let's test your new knowledge in a little who, what, when, where, why, and how quiz. Feel free to look back in the text to find the answers if you need to, but try to remember first!

1 What was Ruth's religion?

→ A Catholic

→ B Jewish

→ C Buddhist

→ D Mormon

2 Where was Ruth born?

→ A Detroit, Michigan

→ B San Francisco, California

→ C Brooklyn, New York

→ D Stockholm, Sweden

3 What were her nickname, birth name, and "school name" as a child (in that order)?

→ A Kiki, Joan, and Ruth

→ B Joan, Kiki, and Ruth

→ C Ruth, Kiki, and Joan

→ D Celia, Marilyn, and Ruth

4 Who was Ruth's husband?

→ A Antonin Scalia

→ B Robert E. Cushman

→ C Vladimir Nabokov

→ D Marty Ginsburg

5 What were some of Ruth's greatest accomplishments?

→ A Running a marathon, composing classical music, flying an airplane

→ B Winning a horseback riding ribbon, climbing Mount Everest, baking a cake

→ C Selling a house, surfing a big wave, becoming a mayor

→ D Becoming the second woman and the first Jewish woman to serve on the United States Supreme Court, changing laws so women and men received equal rights, directing the Women's Rights Project for the American Civil Liberties Union

6 When did Ruth attend Cornell University?

→ A 1950 to 1954

→ B 1990 to 1994

→ C 2010 to 2014

→ D 1933 to 1937

7 What year did Ruth graduate from Columbia Law School?

→ A 1989

→ B 1993

→ C 1959

→ D 2019

8 Why did Ruth sometimes wear a special collar when reading a Supreme Court decision?

→ A When she was excited about the court's decision

→ B When she read a dissent, or disagreement, with the court's decision

→ C When she was afraid she made the wrong decision

→ D When she was going to sing the decision to opera music

9 What was Ruth's first job after law school?

→ A Clerking for Judge Edmund Palmieri

→ B Teaching kindergarten

→ C Waiting tables at a restaurant

→ D Being president of the ACLU

10 **Who chose Ruth for the United States Court of Appeals for the District of Columbia, and who chose her for the Supreme Court?**

→ A President Obama and President Clinton

→ B President Carter and President Clinton

→ C President Washington and President Lincoln

→ D President George H. Bush and President Grant

11 **How did Ruth change the law and the world for women?**

→ A Making sure women got a chance to cook

→ B Making sure women could vote

→ C Making sure women got equal pay with the Lilly Ledbetter Fair Pay Act

→ D Making sure women could be president

Answers: 1. B; 2. C; 3. A; 4. D; 5. D; 6. A; 7. C; 8. B; 9. A; 10. B; 11. C

Our World

How did Ruth's work change our world today and make a difference in the lives of millions of people? Let's look at a few things that have happened because of Ruth Bader Ginsburg.

→ Between 1993 and 2013, the number of female college professors grew by more than 375,000. Now students can learn from teachers with **diverse** points of view and life experiences. More female professors also means more research on issues that affect women.

→ In 1963, women made 59 cents to every dollar men made. Now, on average, women who work full time make 80 cents to every dollar men make. That's not yet equal pay for equal work, but it's progress. Furthermore, a boss today can't refuse to hire someone just because she is a woman. Hopefully, someday soon, everyone will get equal pay for equal work.

→ Thanks to Ruth, a **jury** in a court is now made up of a group that represents your peers. Ruth argued that women should not be left out of juries, but she also argued that people of color should have jurors who reflect them, too. The goal of these changes was to make juries more fair, so they won't decide someone is guilty (or innocent) just because of their gender or race.

JUMP IN THE THINK TANK FOR MORE!

Now let's think a little more about what RBG did, the ways she changed our world, and how those changes affect the world we live in.

→ How has Ruth's work made a difference in your life, or the lives of the women in your world?

→ Why did Ruth decide to take on cases that seemed to be discriminating against men, not just women?

→ How do you think you benefit from the advances Ruth helped make happen?

Glossary

anti-Semitism: The act of disliking or unfair treatment of people because they are Jewish

appeal: The act of asking a higher court to reverse the decision of a lower court

conservative: The thought process of staying true to existing ideas, laws, and ways of operating rather than taking on new ones. In America, a conservative usually believes that more of the power to make and enforce laws should belong to the individual states.

Constitution of the United States: A document written in 1787 right after the United States first became a country, which states the basic laws of how the country must be run

controversial: Describing a topic many people disagree about

court: A place where legal cases are heard and decided

discrimination: The unfair treatment of different categories of people, based on where they come from, what they look like, what religion they are, or if they are male or female

dissent: The act of disagreeing with the opinion of the majority. In the Supreme Court, a dissent is written and presented alongside the case's final decision.

diverse: A group with a lot of variety, so not everything or everyone is the same

equal rights: The act of giving all people the same treatment, opportunities, responsibilities, and freedoms

gender discrimination: The act of treating people unfairly because they identify as male or female

gender equality: The act of treating people fairly and making sure they have equal rights and opportunities regardless of whether they identify as male or female

immigrant: A person born in one country but who has moved to another country

injustice: An act or behavior that's not fair, right, or equal

inspired: The desire to take action in response to something you have seen, heard, or experienced

judge: The person who rules on legal cases in a court

judicial code: The laws that govern a particular land or country

jury: A group of ordinary citizens who are chosen to decide in a trial case whether an accused person is guilty or innocent of a crime

justice: Fairness; also, "justice" can refer to one of the member panel of judges who makes decisions on the Supreme Court

justify: To prove why something is right and fair

lawsuit: A dispute between people or groups of people that's brought to a court to decide. "To sue" is to bring a lawsuit against someone.

lawyer: A person who has studied the law and can represent other people or groups of people in court

liberal: The thought process of being open to new ideas, laws, and ways of operating. In America, a liberal usually believes more of the power to make and enforce laws should belong to the national government.

social justice: The act of making wealth, opportunities, and privileges within a society more fair and equal for everyone

Supreme Court: The highest court in the United States. The Supreme Court is made up of nine justices, who are some of the most accomplished lawyers and judges in the country. Being on the Supreme Court is a lifelong job—you can't get fired.

tenure: The act of having a permanent job position, where one cannot be fired or let go

trailblazer: A person who is the first to do something, an innovator

Bibliography

Above the Law. Accessed September 2, 2019. www.abovethelaw.com.

American Civil Liberties Union. "Tribute: The Legacy of Ruth Bader Ginsburg and WRP Staff." Accessed September 2, 2019. www.aclu.org/other/tribute-legacy-ruth-bader-ginsburg-and-wrp-staff.

Chittal, Nisha and Bridget Todd. "9 Powerful Ruth Bader Ginsburg Quotes." MSNBC.com. February 16, 2015. www.msnbc.com/msnbc/9-powerful-ruth-bader-ginsburg-quotes.

Columbia Alumni. "Associate Justice Ruth Bader Ginsburg at She Opened the Door, Columbia University Women's Conference." YouTube. February 22, 2018. www.youtube.com/watch?v=tQHxxnThDxg.

Economy, Peter. "17 Powerfully Inspiring Quotes from Ruth Bader Ginsburg." Inc.com. January 12, 2019. www.inc.com/peter-economy/17-powerfully-inspiring-quotes-from-ruth-bader-ginsburg.html.

Ginsburg, Ruth Bader, Mary Hartnett, and Wendy W. Williams. *My Own Words*. New York: Simon & Schuster, 2016.

Ginsburg, Ruth Bader and Anders Bruzelius. *Civil Procedure in Sweden.* The Hague: Martinus Nijhoff, 1965.

Ginsburg, Ruth Bader, Kenneth M. Davidson, and Herma Hill Kay. *Sex Based Discrimination: Text, Cases, and Materials.* Eagan, Minnesota: West Publishing Company, 1974.

Huffington Post. "Radcliffe Day 2015." June 17, 2015. www.radcliffe.harvard.edu/video/radcliffe-day-2015-justice-ruth-bader-ginsburg.

Knight, Louise. "The 19th-Century Powerhouse Who Inspired RBG." CNN. Last modified September 1, 2018. www.cnn.com/2018/09/01/opinions/ruth-bader-ginsburg-rbg-and-grimke-sisters-louise-knight/index.html.

National Partnership for Women and Families. "America's Women and the Wage Gap." May 2019. www.nationalpartnership.org/our-work/resources/workplace/fair-pay/americas-women-and-the-wage-gap.pdf.

Notorious. Directed by Julie Cohen and Betsy West. New York: CNN, 2018.

On the Basis of Sex. Directed by Daniel Stiepleman. Los Angeles: Universal Pictures Home Entertainment, 2019.

Acknowledgments

I want to thank RBG for being such an inspiration and an honor to write about. I appreciate my outstanding editor, Orli, who entrusted me with this book and guided me with grace, precision, and determination. I appreciate my parents, Janice and Ray, for their encouragement. To my brother, Steve, the tax attorney, who advised on the legalese—thanks! Kudos to my talented writers' group—Andrew, Brandi, Evan, Kyle, and Sonia. In memory of my Grandma Grace, my Aunt Judy, and my mentor, Ilse. To my nephews: Sam, Jacob, and David, and my niece, Sofia. Thanks to the entire Callisto team! I am supported by family and friends: Michelle G., Susan, Ann, Greg, Danielle, Jeanne, Deborah, Laurie, Tanya, Carla, Julia, Ira, Maureen, Amparo, Michael, Ricardo, Alejandra, Arden, Jen, Tami, Karen, Annie, Crystal, Bryan, Jessica, Marji, Marcy, Lara, Anita, Bob, Jerry, Nena, Mel, Jami, Stacy, Rick, Michelle R., Chalmers, Violeta, Diana, Juanca, and Sylvia Boorstein.

—SBK

About the Author

SUSAN B. KATZ is an award-winning, bestselling bilingual author, National Board Certified Teacher, educational consultant, and keynote speaker. She taught for over 25 years. Susan has 10 published books, and 15 forthcoming, with Scholastic, Random House, Rockridge Press, and Barefoot Books. *Meditation Station* (Bala Books/Shambhala), a book about trains and mindfulness, won the 2020 International Book Award for Best Mind/Body/Spirit Children's Book. Some of her other titles include: *ABC, Baby Me!*, *My Mama Earth* (Moonbeam Gold Award Winner for Best Picture Book and named Top Green Toy by Education.com), *ABC School's for Me* (illustrated by Lynn Munsinger), and *All Year Round*, which she translated into Spanish as *Un Año Redondo* for Scholastic. She also authored *The Story of Frida Kahlo*, *The Story of Jane Goodall*, *The Story of Albert Einstein*, *The Story of Marie Curie*, *The Story of Gandhi*, and *The Story of Fred Rogers* for Rockridge Press. *The Story of Ruth Bader Ginsburg* hit #18 on the overall Amazon Bestseller List and #9 among all kids' books. Susan is also the executive director of ConnectingAuthors.org, a national nonprofit bringing children's book authors and illustrators into schools. She served as the strategic partner manager for authors at Facebook. When she's not writing, Susan enjoys traveling, salsa dancing, and spending time at the beach. You can find out more about her books and school visits at **SusanKatzBooks.com.**

About the Illustrator

MICAH PLAYER is an author and illustrator of books and games for children. He studied graphic design at the University of Utah in Salt Lake City before moving to Southern California to work in the apparel industry where he designed graphics for clothing, gifts, and accessories. His first picture book, *Chloe, Instead,* was published by Chronicle Books in 2012. He lives in a little house beneath a giant tree in the mountains of Utah with a lovely schoolteacher named Stephanie. They are the parents of two rad kids, one brash little Yorkshire Terrier, and several Casio keyboards. His work can be found at **MicahPlayer.com**.